Inspiration

FOR DAILY LIFE

Poems and prayers that spark:
Salvation, Godly Wisdom, Peace, Love, Hope

SHIRLEY A. HOWARD

INKS & BINDINGS

Copyright © 2023 by Shirley A. Howard

ISBN: 979-8-88615-120-6 (Paperback)

979-8-88615-121-3 (E-book)

Inks and Bindings
888-290-5218
www.inksandbindings.com
orders@inksandbindings.com

Contents

Part 1: God Reveals Himself To Us
- God:
  - o Calls us
  - o Blesses us
  - o Assures us of His power
  - o Is our peace
  - o Gives us sight
  - o Gives freedom
  - o Is faithful and true
  - o Helps us set our life pace
  - o Directs our way
  - o Gives us purpose and is gracious
  - o Embraces us in His arms
  - o Is love

Part 2: Rise Above Your Circumstances
- When you:
  - o Listen for God's voice
  - o Trust Him at all times
  - o Cry out to Him
  - o Always wait on God
  - o Beware of time as you move to the future
  - o Don't worry; God controls all
  - o Know that life is a journey of faith
  - o Know that pray is key
  - o At a crossroad, stand still
  - o Trust God to finish strong
  - o Know that God is excellent

Part 3: Prayers Of Praise And Gratitude
- o Christ lives within
- o He draws us near
- o Give God thanks at all times
- o Focus on God's goodness
- o Totally trust and rely on Him
- o God reveals hidden and secret things
- o Freedom in His love, peace, and joy
- o Reflect upon God's grace, mercy, protection, and provisions
- o God is our Healer, Friend, Divine Promise Keeper
- o God is amazing, eternal, and immortal

Part 4: Intimate Worship
o Waiting on God
o Embrace His Holy Presence
o Know His voice
o God gives us purpose
o We trust and obey Him
o We are abundantly blessed
o He is the Source of our supply
o Life's trials can't hold us down

Part One

God Reveals Himself to us

A Call To Serve

A call to serve, we do not deserve!
But out of God's love, He extends the call!
He is there for us, whether we succeed or fail!

Trust the Lord and obey—watch His grace and
Mercy prevail! He won't allow the devil and
His demons to assail!

Trust the Lord and obey; and He will guide each
Step of your way! Study, fast, and pray; ask Him
To order your steps every day!

(Mk. 10:45; Rom. 12:10)

Bless My Soul

Lord, bless my soul, for the half hasn't
Been told! One day, I'll walk the streets
Paved in clear gold!

To You, Jesus, I'm eternally sold! On
Your truth and righteousness, I stand
Holy, yet bold!

For, one day, Your glorious face, I'll
Behold; as You welcome me to Your
Holy fold!

Thank You Jesus! Thank You Lord!
I'm a blessed and happy soul!

(Nu. 6:24-26; Phil. 4:7, 19; Eph. 1:3;
3 Jn. 1:2)

Where You Are

Where you are, oh Lord, is where I desire to be!
It's Your glory that I delight to see!

When You came into my heart, You set me free!
At that moment, Your Spirit declared to my spirit—
Go and be!

You've given me strength and power to walk in
Holy and joyful jubilee! I'm learning to walk in divine
Ecstasy!

Where You are, my Jesus, is where I'll be in person,
One day! To You, I daily pray!

For, You will allow my will and way to desire and do
All that You say! Your commands, I will obey!

Where you are, oh God, is interwoven in my heart
And soul! In You, I'm being made more holy and
Bold!

So, of Your wisdom and greatness, to others, it will
Be told! I anticipate the streets paved in clear gold!

Where I am is where you are, because You live in
Me! You give my blinded eyes sight to see! Where
You are, I declare liberty and victory! I praise You
Lord! I love You and thank You!

(Jer. 29:11; Heb. 6:15; Ps. 57:2; 119:10-11)

Your Peace

Lord Jesus, we thank You for Your peace!
You came! You left! You gave us Your abiding
Peace!

Faith and trust in You is where we place our belief!
From trouble, trials and tests, only You give hope
And sweet relief!

There is no reason to worry or stress! In all these
Things, they serve to bring forth our heart's best!

Your peace, You give it, as long as we live! By the
Holy Spirit, we are sealed!

You fill our empty heart and soul! You remind us
That we are valued members of Your *holy fold*!

To Your holy will and divine way, we're eternally sold!
You strengthen us to stand bold!

To Your Word of Truth, and by fervent prayer, loyal love
To You, we declare!

Your peace brings joy and hope! It assures us in all
That life holds, You give us power to victoriously
Cope!

Hallelujah! Thank You Lord for Your never-ending
Love and ever-abiding peace! Jesus, we love You!

(Jn. 3:16; 14:27; Phil. 4:8)

Open Blinded Eyes

Lord, You specialize in setting captives free!
You open blinded eyes so they can see!
You offer sin-captives their liberty!

You show them how Your Word of Truth is
There to advise! Even in times of trials, You
Reveal truths that were once disguised!

But, because tests are designed to draw
Captives closer to God, trials are a valued prize!

Lord, continue to open blinded eyes! For, only
You can! Reveal Your holy plan! Allow our wish
To become Your command!

Lord, eyes are opened when repentant souls decide
To work Your plan, as You demand, in Jesus' name!

(Matt. 21:14; Mk. 8:22-25; Jn. 9:25; Isa. 29:18)

Faithful And True

I want to be faithful and true!
Lord, I want to be more like You!

Please show and teach me what to
Do! You come to my aid and rescue!
Lord, thank You!

Faithful and true—this is the essence
Of wonderful You!

I go and tell the world who You are!
Jesus, You are the Bright and Morning
Star!

Your love drew me near when I was once
Far! I long to be wherever You are!

For, one day, I'll behold You face to face!
It's all because of Your amazing grace!

(Ps. 9:9-10; 1 Cor. 1:9; 1 Jn. 1:9; Rev. 19:11)

Slow Me Down

Lord, slow me down, so I'll stop and reflect
As I look around! Please allow Your Holy
Spirit, my soul, to perfect!

All sins and unrighteousness, Your Spirit, will
Detect; and by Your grace and mercy, all sins
You'll deflect!

It is the blood of Jesus that makes us perfect
In Your marvelous sight!

Lord, You give us strength to fight the *good fight—*
You empower us to live right!

Lord God, You inspire a new spiritual appetite!
You give us power to win the spiritual fight! Your
Will and way are my heart's delight!

Lord, slow me down! My hope, peace, and joy in
You alone are found!

Thank You Lord! Thank You Jesus! I love You
With all my heart!

(Ps. 27:13-14; 33:20-22; Prov. 3:5-6; Isa. 40:31)

Show Me

Lord, show me what to do!
Show me which direction to go!

I'm stressed and pressed on every side!
This strain and turmoil, I can't hide!

Please come along side—allow Your
Peace and hope to abide! Cleanse me
From the inside!

I resolve, oh God—where You lead, I'll
Allow You to guide! Every need, I trust
You to provide!

Lord, show me which path to take! Help
Me avoid needless mistakes, for Your
Name sake!

Help me to remain faithful and true—to
Avoid all that's fake!

Extend to me Your holy hand! I'll take it so
That, a faithful, loving, and kind soldier of
The cross, I'll make!

Lord, show me! Then I'll become more
Like You, in Jesus' name! I love You!

(Ps. 25:4-5; 16:11; 37:23; 119:105; Prov. 3:5-6)

Let Me Live

Lord, let me live! Each day, my life to You,
I give!

Teach me! And I'll teach others how to live,
Love, and forgive!

Just let me live! I glance my eyes to Golgotha's
Hill! For all humanity, You struck the eternal
Deal!

Jesus, You hung, bleed, and died! And upon
You, the sins of the world were tried!

Your love and faithfulness, to all humanity,
Cannot be denied! By faith, the Holy Spirit
Came to live inside!

You delight to order our steps—each day You
Are there to lead us and guide!

Lord let me live! My life to You, I choose to
Give for as long as I live!

(Jn. 14:6-7; Phil. 1:21-24; Gal. 2:20)

Your Grace

Lord, Your grace surrounds! It picks me up when
I'm down! It gives me courage and strength to fight
The *good fight*—to challenge evil and hate in every
Round!

By Your amazing grace, to love and forgive, I'm
Faithfully bound! Your love and kindness won't let
Me down!

Your grace holds my hand! The Holy Spirit reveals
God's mighty plan! He teaches me to do all I can!
I choose to follow the Savior's divine commands!

Dear Lord, Your grace shelters me from the storms
Of life! I'm bathed, fed, and led by Your loving and
Radical grace!

Jesus, it's by Your grace that I have a resting and
Eternal place in Your Holy Presence forevermore!

For, with Your own suffering and shed blood, You
Opened eternal salvation's door! And of Your love
And hope, we hunger for You more and more!

(Ephesians 2:8-9)

In Your Loving Arms

In your loving arms I experience peace and calm!
Your indwelling Holy Spirit protects me from harm!

In You, Jesus, I'm given strength and wisdom to
Overcome! I worship and thank You for all the
Troubles and problems You've brought me from!

In Your Word and fervent prayer, I experience holy
Reform!

In Your loving arms, Jesus, I'm protected from the
Enemy of my soul! One day, I'll walk on the streets
Of clear gold!

Even now, You empower me to serve You; and on
Your truth—stand bold!

In Your loving arms, You bless my soul! To You
Jesus, I'm eternally sold! I love and praise You!

(Ps. 98:1; Isa. 41:10; 59:1; Jn. 3:16)

I Love You

I love You Jesus—I really do!
I yield all that I am to wonderful You!

You are Almighty God—the faithful
One so gracious and true!

Teach me to be like You—to live and
Love others as you tell us to!

For, we are known by the love we have
For one another! We must be willing
To serve and sacrifice for each other!

I love You Jesus! But You loved me
More! Blessings after blessings, over
My life, You continually pour!

You daily lead and guide Your children
To Your peaceful shore!

Eternal life, joy, and hope, You give now
And forevermore! Jesus, I love You—
I really do! Thank You!

(Jn. 3:16; Mk. 12:30)

Jesus Stands

Jesus stands at the door of your heart!
Open it and let Him in, so a new life will begin!

He welcomes you with peace and joy within! He
Died and rose to forgive sins! Let unfaithfulness
End!

Jesus stands and knocks! His plans for your life,
He commands—but He won't force your hand!

Let the Savior in! His specialty is to take away
Sins; and give peace and hope that your spirit will
Comprehend!

Today is a great day to begin! For your cause,
Eternal life, He came to defend!

But you must invite Him in! And each day He
Stands at the door of your heart! Hear Him knock!

Jesus is the true and living God! He won't leave
You when life gets hard! Let Him in!

He's there to keep you from falling apart! He
Stands and knocks at your heart—invite Him in!
He takes away confessed sin!

(Jn. 3:16; Rev. 3:20)

From The Prison To The Palace

(A Rap)

From the prison to the palace
Is what God did!
It wasn't that Joseph Was a whiz
But that he— did God's biz!

From the prison to the palace
I do believe—
From God's hand— you too can receive!

My brother— my sister—Listen to me!
Trust in Jesus and He will make you free~

From the prison to the palace
He will show— What you can be!

From the prison to the palace
Just give God praise!

Unchartered trails
He'll help you blaze
What God can do
You'll stand amazed!

From the prison to the palace
He'll take you there
Look around and you will see
That God is everywhere!

From the prison to the palace
Just give God praise—with both hands raised!

(Genesis 41:14-24)

Part Two

Rise Above Your Circumstances

You Carry Us

Each day, You carry us in Your arms!
You lead and guide, as You protect
Us from harm!

You speak, and there is peace and
Calm! You assure us there is no
Reason for alarm!

Each day we awake, You invite all to
Come! The indwelling Holy Spirit,
Transforms! Our soul and spirit, to
God's will begin to conform!

Lord, You carry us each and every
Day! So, we can't help but give You
Worship and praise!

Thank You, Lord, for leading and
Guiding us all our days! In all You do
For and in us, we are fully amazed!
Thank You Lord! Glory hallelujah to
Your Mighty Name!

(Ps. 91:1; Dt.31:6; Heb. 13:5)

A Blessed Day

This has been a blessed day!
Lord, I'm looking to You to guide
My way!

You spoke to me throughout this
Day with seeds of blessings
Thrown around, as Your glory
Fell down!

This is a blessed day! I heard You
Say: *Hold on, don't quit! Give the
Devil a fit!*

Burdened down and bowed to the
Ground is where the devil's work is
Found!

Suppressed and oppressed is the
Work that he does best!

But the more trust there is in God,
Satan's hold become less and less!

It's a blessed day when we choose
To walk in God's straight and narrow
Way!

By faith, I choose to lift up my bowed
Down head!

This is a blessed day! For I'm totally
Sold out to God's holy way!
So, in His presence and under His
Holy power, I'll stay!

No longer bowed down in bondage's
Grip—I stand holy and bold due to
Faith's tip: *Trust God and obey!*

Thank You Lord for this blessed day!
Guide my feet in Your holy way!

(Jer. 17:7-8)

In Dark Times

We live in dark times! This world is corrupt
With crimes of all kinds!

But in all things, even out of confusion, the
Spirit of God removes doubts and delusions!

By His Guiding Light, you are able to draw on
Wisdoms way—God's conclusion!

In dark times and in all times—totally trust in Holy
God! Allow Him to control and soften your hard
And weary heart!

And from the darkness within this world, He will
Lead you by His Light of salvation and love!

Allow Jesus to transform your thoughts and heart,
So that in the dark times, you'll still see and walk
In His Holy Light that eternally burns!

And in dark times and in all times, confess and
Forsake your sins! Reflect the light that God placed
Within!

Go! And tell others of the Light of God that shines
Brightest in the dark times, by His design!

(Eph. 5:8; 2 Cor.4:6; Jn.1:5; 1 Pet. 2:9; Acts 26:18)

Crying Out

Oh Lord, my heart and my soul cry out to
You! I long to do all You tell me to!

When I consider all You brought me through,
I desire to spend eternity with You!

You come to my aid and rescue! Your Word
And Holy Spirit reveal what is holy and true!

Oh Lord, I'm so in love with You! And for
Everything You do—THANK YOU!

You fill me with Your Holy Spirit over and over
Again! You take away all my sins!

Your grace and mercy cleanse me from within!
Eternal life with You will never end!

I cry out day and night! In faith, I wage the good
Fight!

Your goodness and compassion teach me to
Do what is right in Your holy sight!

By faith, I cry out to rise above the fear and doubt!
It reveals God's holy clout!

In earnest, against evil, I fight and fight! The Holy
Spirit allows me to win each bout!

Over and over, I continue to cry out! Lord, You
Hear my cry! And of this fact, I have no doubt!

Thank You Jesus! Thank You Lord! Thank You
Holy Spirit for hearing and responding when I
Cry out!

(Ps. 18:6; 34:4; 120:1; 142:1-7; Isa. 59:1)

I Wait On You

Lord, I wait on You!
Show me what I need to do!

You are always near—You come
To my rescue! Your Word is true!

You take away my doubt and fear—
You draw me near!

You turn my sadness into cheer!
You make cloudy thoughts clear!

I wait on wonderful You!
You whisper and tell me what I
Need to do!

Lord, I wait on miraculous You!
Move Lord, and perform the miracles
That only You can do!

I'll tell of Your love and goodness to
All—this duty is Your holy call for us
All!

I love You! I wait on You! You are
Always faithful and true! And for all
That You do and say—thank You!

(Dt. 31:8; Ps. 27:14; 2 Pet. 3:9; Isa. 30:18)

A Crucial Hour

At this time in your life, this is a
Crucial hour! Will you believe and
Serve God, or yield to the devil's
Power?

Lies and deceptions are all the
Enemy has! Through fear, doubt,
And wayward thoughts, he tries to
Prevent us from doing what we
Ought!

Trust and obey Jesus Christ the
Holy God; and live by the precept
He taught—*when you are weak,
Then you are strong!*

"You are more than a conqueror!"
"Don't be afraid, just believe!"

Things are not as they seem! God
Delights and protects His redeemed!

Trust God in this crucial hour; and
Your eyes will see! You'll experience
His miraculous power!

This is your time! This is your
Defining hour! Stand up for God!
Give Him all your heart!

Then go—and with the rod of faith
Your 'dead sea' will part, in Jesus'
Name! Amen!

(Jn. 3:16; Rom. 8:37; 2 Cor. 4:18; 12:8-10)

The Sun Is Going Down

The clouds of adversity keep rolling in as we near
Our journey's end!

For, the sun is going down! It's difficult to see the
Dangers that surround!

Life has taught us that the love and protection of
God, for the redeemed, are found!

Trust, believe, and serve God with your whole
Heart! His presence will never depart! God's Word
Reveals His heart!

Though the sun is going down, yet in the heat of
The final battle, God will fight each round!

For, His eternal love and provisions are found! And
Forever with the setting of the sun, the *Son-shine of
God"* is always found!

Don't worry or be fearful! For, the sun is going down
In every life! Jesus Christ, God's Son, paid the
Ultimate price!

Open your eyes and your heart, see the provisions
Given by the shedding of Christ's blood!

Jesus is the Living Word! He died and rose for our
Sins! New life and hope with Him begins!

The sun is going down! Only in Jesus Christ is
Eternal life found! Come to Jesus while you still
Have time!

For, the sun is going down; yet the *Son of God* still
Extends His welcoming hand and says—*come!*
Come to Jesus before the setting of the sun!

(Jn. 3:16; 2 Cor. 4:6; Ps. 84:11; Isa. 9:2)

From Now To The Next

As I move from the now to the next,
It's by Your Holy Spirit that I connect!

Daily, I trust and obey You, so that
Your Spirit will, my soul and spirit,
Correct!

It's through Your Holy Word and prayer
That I start to perfect my way of life by
How I live and treat my fellow man!

Lord teach me how to live out, in real
Time, Your Holy Commands!

I extend my hand to take Your hand, as
You move me from the old way of 'now'
Living to the 'next'—Kingdom living!

For, in the 'next', it's all about You and
The Kingdom!

Lord, teach me how to win souls for
Eternity! Show me how to love people
Into Your Kingdom! Give me Your heart!

Help me live so people will see the Jesus
In me; and be drawn to Your goodness,
Kindness, and love!

Lord move me from 'now' to 'next'—in
Jesus Name, I stake this claim! This is
My prayer!

Don't

Don't worry! Don't be afraid! Trust and obey
God! Know that He will come to your aid!

He sees every choice and decision that you've
Made! His plans to give you a hope and a future
Are already laid!

Don't turn from God; but to His love, entrust
Your heart! For, He holds you in high regard!

Don't worry or fret! Don't allow unexpected and
Unforeseen things make you upset!

Don't give up or quit! But at God's mercy seat,
Humbly sit! Cry out to God until your holy fire is
Lit!

With all that's within you, give it to Jesus! Just
Make up your mind—*I don't have to quit and I
Won't! Help me, Lord! Thank You! I love You!
It's done in Jesus' Name!*

(Matt. 6:25-27; Jer. 29:11)

An Empty Spot

There was an empty spot within my heart
That can only be filled by Holy God!

It's the spot that keeps me from falling apart!
It holds the reigns of my eternal soul!

This reserved spot purges me! It makes me
Humble, yet whole, as it cleanses my soul, body,
And; it molds!

This empty spot was designed by Creator God—
It resides within the human being, where only He
Can fill! A spot where the Holy Spirit seals!

By faith and trust in Jesus Christ, the redeemed
Must believe so that everlasting salvation they'll
Receive!

I'm *now* complete and whole in body, spirit, and soul!
For, the Holy Spirit of God rules and reigns in my life,
As He controls!

A once empty spot is now filled with His eternal love,
Grace, and mercy! And also, filled with God's eternal
Peace and unending hope!

Allow God to fill your empty spot! In Jesus' name
Stake your claim!

(Eph. 5:18; 1 Cor. 6:19)

Journey Of Faith

The way of God is a journey of faith!
But our own way is one of haste!

We want to set our own pace! Yet,
We desire God's grace without seeking
His face!

Lord, each day You allow trials and
Tests to teach us that only by faith can
We win the race!

The journey of faith can be a testing and
Trying place! Yet, God's Spirit gives us
Strength wrapped in His mercy and grace!

On this journey of faith, know that Jesus
Is on the case! Keep pressing as you
Patiently pray!

By faith we will stay, when the Holy Word,
We obey! Faith will pave the way!

The journey of faith is lived out each day—
Fast, study, patiently, and diligently pray!

Sense the Spirit of God moving within your
Heart! And your way will become
Increasingly clear—

He banishes doubt and fear! So, patiently
Wait on God! Faith is a journey that requires
Time—so, to the love of Jesus, rest and
Consign!

Keep your trust in Jesus—the holy, faithful,
And divine—make sure that He is your God!

(Heb. 11:6)

Jesus Saves

Jesus died on a cross and rose—He did it
To save lost souls!
Go! Be sure that the gospel story is told!

His grace and mercy shapes and molds;
And lifts sin's heavy load!

To the Savior, a sin debt is owed—give
Your life to Jesus and be saved!

Only Jesus gives us power to conquer
Death and the grave!

The road to everlasting life, with His precious
Blood, is paved!

Look up and live; and by faith, Christ will save!
At the tomb, you'll find an empty grave!

For only by faith and trust in Jesus Christ is one
Saved!

Jesus forever lives; and eternal life, only He
Gives! Praise the Lord; bless His holy name!

(Jn. 3:16; 2 Thess. 1:10; Heb. 4:14-16)

Don't Forget Your Key

Don't forget your key!
Jesus died to set you free!

Upon the cross, He died,
Rose, and purchased your
Liberty!

At Calvary's Hill, Jesus gave
The down payment so that,
By His Spirit, we are filled!

And at the moment of
Redemption, we are sealed
Through trust and obedience!

God heals; and all sins, He
Forgives!

Go! Live for Jesus! He's the
Key! He eternally lives in you;
And came to guide your destiny!

The battle was settled in the
Garden of Gethsemane—*"Father,
Not My will, but Your will be done!"*

Don't forget that Jesus Christ is
The *Eternal Key!* He opens
Blinded eyes so they plainly see!

(Jn. 3:16; 14:6-11; Rev. 1:18)

Stand Still

When you don't know what to do, stand still
And wait! For, the Lord has a Word for you!

Never forget that God is always faithful and
True; even when we disobey what He tells us
To do!

Never question or doubt His loyal love for you!
He has a great plan that He's taking you to!

Stand still when you start to doubt! Cry out to
God! Invite Him to help you work things out!

Stand still! With His Word of Truth, be filled, so
Your faith and trust will build!

With the power of the Holy Spirit stay filled! Never
Forget that by His Spirit, you've been sealed!

For it's a one time and eternal deal! Stand still!
Trust and obey the Lord! Wait on Him!

In God's timing, He will reveal His plan and purpose!
So, until then, be still! But do pray, and by the Holy
Spirit, be filled!

Serve and share the Gospel story! Tell the world
About His glory!

Be still! Be energized and filled with His power—go
Share it in Jesus' Name! Praise God!

(Ps. 46:10)

Butterfly

Oh Lord, like a butterfly from its cocoon
Deliver me from this mess soon and
Very soon!

Let the beauty of Your Word be
Reverently applied and heard!

People are blinded by selfish
Ambition, ignorance, and greed!

It's because on Your Holy and
Righteous Word, they do not feed!

Like a butterfly, allow me to come
Forth with colors bright—trusting and
Relying on You to win the fight!

And by faith and trust in You, I take
Flight as I'm maintaining and sustaining
By Your holy might!

Like a butterfly let me show forth the
Beauty of You, so to others, I tell and
Show forth evidence of Your mighty
Rescue!

Like a moth to a flame, allow Your
People to desire change. For the devil
Appears to be winning the game!

Like a butterfly allow me to fly, displaying
Your beauty everywhere by revealing to
Unsuspecting souls the enemy's snare!

Like a butterfly, Lord, let me fly into Your
Arms and be filled with peace, joy, and
Calm far above the dangers and snares
Of this world!

Like a butterfly let Your beauty and
Strength be seen in me until the day that
I die—so Your name, I will glorify!

Ps. 139:7-10, 23-24)

It's Being Done

It's being done—all that you asked for will come
Forth at last!
So, don't be discouraged by the mistakes and the
Outcomes from the past!

Keep the faith! Don't forget—only what you do
For Christ will last!

Don't allow your spirit to stay downcast! Look
Up to your God with gratitude in your heart!

Some things you suffered were for your good, to
Teach you to live as you should! Did you really live
The best that you could?

With Christ, you can't fail! Time and obedient faith
Will tell! Trust God and obey!

Drink from His Living well! Be filled with the Holy
Spirit of God—receive Him and know His heart!

Your deliverance from the enemy's grasp is loosed!
Heaven's glow is produced!

Walk in God's love, joy, peace, and power! It's
Given to you in this hour!

The windows of Heaven are open! Your Lord and
God has spoken! His manifested power and
Goodness, within you, is the token!

Go! Serve as God commands! In His name, execute
His plan! For God trusts you because you trust Him
In all you face—a mystery of God's amazing and
Radical grace!

It's being done! God commands and demands—
Go forth in His power and love, and serve! For, all you
Asked God for is already done—victory is won!

(Heb. 11:1-2, 6; Jam. 1:2-8; Jude 22-23)

Finish Strong

Lord, I continue to fight the good fight; so as to
Finish my course by keeping the faith to finish
Strong!

Lord, within my heart, You've given a melody and
A praise song!

For, upon an old rugged cross, Your body was
Hung; so that over sin, death, and the grave, we'd
Have power to overcome!

Help me finish strong, even when the trials and
Tests of life, seek to render, my life, undone!

Only by faith and trust in Jesus Christ will victory
Be won! And all the trials of faith, be successfully
Done!

Even with the uncertainty and unexplained
Situations of life, You help me to finish strong!

In the midst of prayer, You give me a new worship
And praise song!

All that I do and say on this journey let it be done
To glorify You! For, my heart's desire is to finish
Strong in Jesus' name!

(Ps. 34:7; Acts 20:17-24; 2 Tim. 4:7-8)

Excellent

Oh Lord, my Lord, how excellent
Is Your name!

You came to earth to give us
Second birth!

I love You Jesus, but You loved
Me first—You alone quench my
Spiritual thirst!

Oh how wonderful You are! For
You were once far, but for love,
You came near!

You allow us, who trust; to rise
Above doubt and fear—with new
Eyes, we see things clear!

It's your Holy Name that I revere!
Your love compels me to bow
Before You, joyful and sincere!

Oh how excellent is Your name!
All who truly know You can't
Remain the same!

My eternal loyalty and obedience
To You, Jesus, I claim!

Oh how excellent You are! How
Excellent is Your Holy and
Righteous name!

(Ps. 8:1-9)

Part Three

Prayers of Praise and Gratitude

Candle Lit

My candle is lit; and I won't quit
So, at Your Mercy Seat, I humbly sit!

I fast, pray, and meditate on the Holy
Writ! I resolve to give the devil a fit!

For, to the will, way, and purpose of
God, I choose to commit!

It's to Your grace, mercy, and love, I
Submit my life—Jesus already paid
Sin's price!

My candle of faith is lit! For the God
I serve is totally legit!

Christ's blood and righteousness gave
Satan the fatal hit—

God gave the redeemed, true grit, and
The power to overcome the devil's pit!

Jesus is the Light; and my candle is
Eternally lit in Christ's love and hope!
Faith and trust in Jesus is the antidote!

(Matt. 5:14-16; Jn. 8:12; 9:5; 12:46; Isa. 42:6)

I Give

Lord, I give my all to You!
Help me learn what You are trying
To teach me!

Please come to my aid and rescue!
Show and teach me what I must do!

Fill me with Your Holy Spirit! A life
That' pleasing to You, help me live it!

You have always been with me, even
When I was unaware! But now, I know
You truly care!

Your love, peace, joy, and hope serve
As an antidote for me to cope

I study the Living Word that the Spirit
Wrote! Each morsel of truth offer peace
And eternal hope!

To You, Jesus, I give all You've given to
Me! For, You open my eyes to truly see!
Thank You!

(1 Chron. 29:14; Ps. 37:4; Prov. 11:25; 18:16)

Draw Me Near

Lord, draw me near! Then the trouble
Around me, I won't fear!

You make cloudy things bright and
Clear! When I'm in need, You come
Near! You spread holy cheer!

You draw me near! Nearer to You I
Daily cling! On my lips, You've given
A song to sing!

Sweet melodies flow from my heart!
They empower me to keep Jesus on
My mind! He is loving and very kind!

Jesus, You are the One true God!
Your Holy Word promises that You will
Never part!

Lord, draw me near! I sense Your holy
Presence that's always near! All my
Days, it's You, Jesus Whom I'll revere!

Draw me near! For, the path I must take
Is clear! I'll tell the world that only Your
Name, cast out doubt and fear! Please
Draw me near in Jesus' name! Amen!

(James 4:8; Ps. 145:18; Col. 3:16; Heb. 10:22)

Thank You Lord

Thank You Jesus! Thank You Lord
For all You are doing! Within me, I'm
Maturing!

My soul and spirit are continually
Growing! Faith and love, the Holy
Spirit is bestowing!

By Your truth, righteousness, and
Faithfulness, *gospel seeds* I'm sowing!
They are scattered by the wind—
Revealing sin!

Salvation, freedom, and deliverance
Are blowing, as the seeds of redemption
Keep going from mouth to mouth, and
From heart to heart!

Thank You Jesus! Thank You Father
God for Your eternal gift! The Holy Spirit
Is the Helper Who enlightens and lifts!

From death and hell to life and Heaven
With Jesus is the eternal gift! Thank You
Lord for all You do! I truly love You!

(Ps. 97:12; 100:4; 105:1; 106:1; Col. 3:15-16; 1
Thess. 5:8)

Quicken My Soul

Lord, You quicken my inner being so that Your
Grace and mercy, I'll keep seeing!

Quicken my soul! Please shape me and mold!
For, I'm cold in the shade, and hot in the sun!

Such feelings are not much fun! So, into Your
Presence, I run! It doesn't take much to render
Me undone!

Lord, let Your will be done! Quicken my soul!
Allow me in every situation—stand bold!

Keep reminding me that I'm a member of Your
Holy fold! For Your truth and righteousness
Must be told!

When You quicken my soul, I'm assured that
I'm a blessed and a redeemed soul!

Your constant love and care are more precious
To me than expensive jewels, silver, and gold!

To You, Jesus, I'm eternally sold—please
Continue to keep and bless as You quicken my
Eternal soul!

All that I am and ever will be, reminds me that
All I am is, to You, owed! You carry my heavy
Load! Thank You! I love You!

Ps. 143:11; 71:2; Jn. 5:21; Rom. 8:11; Eph. 2:1)

Without You

Jesus, I can't live without You!
The truth *be* told—I don't want to!

You are faithful, loving, and kind!
You are the Holy One, so divine!

Your grace and mercy is one of a
Kind! For the Divine Trinity has
Cosigned!

Nobody like You Jesus! You are
The Faithful and True! You come
To our aid and rescue when we
Ask and need You to!

Without You Jesus, there is no
Me—*no nothing*! For hope, peace,
And joy, only You can bring!

You give sad and love-weary hearts
A love song to sing! You cause
Souls to beam!

Without You Jesus, there is no
Destiny; and no dream—no anything!

Without You Jesus, there is nothing
At all! But there is life, love, peace
And hope for all who accept Your call!

You are the Great I AM! You rule and
Will reign over all! We praise Your name!

(Psalm 27:1; John 3:16; 14:6)

Hidden Things

Call on the Lord God; and He will show you
Great and mighty things that you didn't know!

It's through the things that God allows that He
Uses to make you grow!

For, when you trust and obey, His grace, mercy,
And wisdom, He will bestow, even when burdens
Hang low!

God reveals hidden things to those who seek Him!
For, He knows what's ahead and what lies in the
Dark!

So, to the will and purpose of Holy God, you must
Hark! Allow your desires, within His way, to park!

Always remember it is Creator God Who reveals
The profound and hidden things! For God knows
Everything! By faith His wisdom, to our life, He
Will bring!

He gives love, joy, peace, and hope! Even in the
Darkness, He gives all that's needed to faithfully
Cope!

God's love and righteousness is the antidote!
Trust the Lord and obey!

(Dan. 2:22; Jer. 33:3)

My Joy

Jesus, You are my Joy that none can destroy!
Woes, troubles, and trials are a trio that can
Defile! But, the love of Jesus has no guile!

Though faced with opposition, Your power and
Peace allow me to hold my position—I'm a
Child of God!

Jesus is my Joy! The Giver of eternal life that
Produces His *love* and *peace* that join hands
With *hope*!

The love, peace, and hope of God gives
Strength to cope in any situation, trial or test—
You discover that Jesus is the best!

All He offers is superior to *all* the rest! He is
There in every trial and test—no contest!

Trust in God! Put all faith in Jesus! The Holy
Spirit brings exceeding joy that nothing or no one
Can destroy!

Jesus Christ, the Son of the Living God, is my Joy!
I'll give hallelujah, thank You Jesus praise all my
Days! Come to Jesus and allow Him to amaze!

(Ex. 15:2; Ps. 28:8; Neh. 8:10; Jn. 15:11; 1 Thess.
2:19)

Freeing

Lord, You are freeing my soul—
Making me whole; and I'm growing
Strong and bold!

I see You Jesus! I feel Your Holy
Spirit! Your cloud of Glory is spreading
All around!

New peace, new hope and joy are found!
When pressed to the ground—higher
And higher, I'm elevated at each round!

Beware! For, the judgment of Holy God is
Being inflicted on the low-down!

Now reverent fear, faith, and love for God,
Within their heart and mind are found!
By God's power every demon is bound!

The unlimited power of God is totally
Freeing; transforming faithful followers
Into Spirit-filled beings!

Holy Father and Almighty God, thank You
For freeing our spirit and soul!

We will behold Your presence on the
Streets of clear gold! Thank You for
Every blessing and saved soul!

For, all of Your goodness has not been
Told! And to You, Jesus, I'm totally sold!

(Jn. 8:36; Gal. 5:1; 1 Pet. 2:16)

Lord, Teach

The good that I do is to glorify You!
All that I go through is to make me
More like You!

Lord, teach me to walk in Your way
Every day! To point others to Your
Pathway!

Lord, teach me to stay in Your straight
And narrow way; to show others who
Are prone to stray!

Jesus Christ, the Son of God is the
Way, Truth, Life, and eternal Light that
Can't be snuffed out!

Lord, teach me that I have no reason
To fear or doubt—for I stand under the
Umbrella of Your holy clout!

By being faithful and true, God will
Bring us through all trials and tests we
Face—we are protected by God's
Amazing grace!

For, You give Your faithful ones a taste
Of Heaven, on earth; and in Heaven, a
Guaranteed dwelling place!

Thank You God, for Your radical grace;
For love, peace, and hope in all I face!

(Ps. 32:8; 71:17; Isa. 48:17)

You Provide

Lord, You provide! Many times it's in disguise!
For it looks one way, but it can be another!

You teach us to be patient with one another!
Patience and kindness go a long way!

Holy Father, lead and guide my steps in Your
Holy way! Order my steps every day!

You provide! You are on our side! Help us to
Know Your truth and apply it without excuse!

Lord, You provide! From dangers seen and
Unseen, Your hand of protection will guide!

You strengthen me from the inside, as Your
Truth and righteousness abides!

You continually provide! Your Holy Spirit lives
And enlightens us regarding Your truth!

To reject the worship and praise of You, there is
No excuse! We thank You, and love You too!

Lord Jesus, You are all we need! Hungry souls,
You feed! Your truth and righteousness, I choose
To heed!

(Ps. 147:8; Matt. 6:26, 31-33; Phil. 4:19; 2 Pet. 1:3)

Help Me

Lord, help me to become all You desire!
At Your Throne of Grace, I daily inquire!

For, to do as You command is what I plan!
Each day, I take hold of Your mighty hand!

Help me serve others with compassion and love!
Give me Your mind and heart to love as You do!

Within, make me like You! Help me to display
The character of Your truth! Jesus, You are the
Faithful and True!

Help me live a life that pleases You! The trials
I face are designed to fulfill Your holy plan!

For, You order my steps! And by the Holy Spirit,
I'm daily kept!

Each test that You allow is designed to develop
Your holy precepts—to move me out of self; so
Only Your good pleasure is left!

In all that I go through, I rely on You to help! I
Believe and trust You with my whole heart!

Lord, thank You! You were there when I spiritually
Slept!

You wiped away the tears as I wept! By Your
Mercy and grace, I'm continually kept!

Lord God, I trust and rely on You to help! For, I
See You; and I love You too!

And in all that You do, I continually repent: *"Lord,*
Forgive me! Thank You for helping me in each life
Quest! You allow me to pass each one of my tests!"

(Psalm 121:18)

I Believe; Help My Unbelief

Lord, I believe! Please help my unbelief! For, doubt
Causes so much grief!

I trust You to give peace and blessed relief! Jesus,
I trust in all-powerful You!

I wait expectantly for You! In times of need, You
Are the One I come to!

At Your nail-scarred feet, I bow! I wait on Your
Grace and mercy to endow—

To move from one level of grace and mercy to
Another, You show me how!

I do believe! Help my heart and mind to perceive
Your righteousness and truth!

Help me to dismiss every useless and selfish excuse—
For such thinking causes my faith to reduce!

Yet, Your love and faithfulness draw me closer to
Wonderful You!

Lord, I believe! I rely on You to help my unbelief! At
Your Throne of grace, mercy, and love, I bow!

I do believe, but please help with unbelief that sneaks
In as a thief! Thank You Lord, I believe in God deep
Within my heart!

(Mk. 9:23-24; Jn. 3:16)

Let It Rain

Father, oh my Father, just let it rain!
Rain down Your power! Your strongest
Shower—let it rain!

Rain down Your glory—it makes me holy!
I surrender my life to You, wholly!

Let it rain! It banishes the fears, doubts,
And the pains! At the cross Jesus bore
The blame!

By His shed blood and righteousness, He
Took upon Himself, our shame!
Lord, let it rain! Jesus, You are the reason
That eternal life is our gain!

Holy Father, thank You that eternal salvation
Rests in that mighty name—Jesus, the
Christ! He's the only *acceptable sacrifice*!

Let it rain! You give victory even through our
Sorrow and pain! Holy Spirit, You teach us;
And You make the lessons plain!

Only in Jesus Christ is eternal life the
Everlasting gain! It washes away the dirt of
Willful sins; and banishes hate, selfishness
And deceit!

Lord, let it rain until only Your love, goodness
And kindness remain! Let it rain!

Allow Your blessings to overflow! This is the
Means by which faithful hearts will know You
And grow!

Allow Your power and glory to continually flow!
Lord, let it rain! Give us a downpour in Jesus'
Name!

(Song of Songs 2:11-12; Isa. 45:8; 55:10; Hosea 6:3)

Hold Me

Lord, hold me in Your strong arms!
Restore Your peace and calm!
Turn off every alarm!

Into Your Holy Presence, I'm welcomed!
With Your loving arms, You beacon me
To come—

To come and drink from Your Living
Fount! Only what's done for You, and
In Your name will count!

Hold me, Jesus! Hold me close!
Continually fill me with your powerful
Holy Ghost!

I bow at Your feet! I yield to You—the
Utmost! Hold me in Your arms until I
Feel that Your mighty power has come!

For a bond of love and righteousness
Is being formed! You protect from all
Harm! Hold me close!

Thank You, Jesus! Thank You, Lord!
I love You with all my heart! Only You
Are the One True God!

(Isa. 41:10, 13; 46:4; 49:16)

Wrap Me

Lord, wrap me in Your loving arms!
Speak peace and calm!

Lord, wrap me in Your arms! Protect
Me from all harm!

Wrap me in Your strong arms, and
Uphold me in the midst of alarm!
Guide me through life's storm!

Don't allow my imagination, doubts,
And fears to overcome! Speak calm!

The awe and wonder of You, within
My soul and spirit, gives me joyful
Melodies to hum!

Wrap me in Your loving and protective
Arms! Overshadow me—speak
Peaceful calm!

Wrap me in Your arms and I won't be
Afraid! I'll wait in patient hope for Your
Divine escape and antidote!

With confident faith and blessed
Assurance, I know that You won't
Forsake!

And each step toward You, I take, a
Stronger person, within me, You make—

When You wrap me in Your arms,
Divine healing begins, as Your love
And peace flow within!

I'll love and serve You; and will do
Your will to the end! Amen!

(Isa. 41:10; 53:1-12; Jn. 14:3)

A Personal Healing Prayer

Lord God, forgive me of all my sins.
Forgive the ones I'm aware of and the ones
That I'm not aware of. Please touch and heal
My body and my soul!

Heal me from the top of my head to the soles
Of my feet. Heal every part that's in between.
Holy Father, minister Your healing power!

As, You heal me from without; Lord, heal me
From within. Heal my aches and pain. Heal
My mind and heart. Allow me to think Your
Thoughts of loving kindness to all people!

Allow the Fruit of the Spirit to grow in me: *love,*
Joy, peace, patience, kindness, goodness,
Faithfulness, gentleness, and self-control.
For these are the makings of a blessed soul!

Lord, touch my emotions with compassion to
Respond with loving concern and not with
Bitter anger and hate. Allow me to reach out
In genuine love that comes from Heaven above!

Take away malice of any kind. Erase every
Hint of jealousy and envy. Don't allow me to
Hold a grudge toward anyone!

Finally, Lord, help me to forgive and extend
Love to those who hate and seek to hurt me.
And the wrong that I do, please forgive me,
As I learn to forgive myself!

Heal every part of me, Lord. Heal my body
From the inside and out. Heal me so that I
May heal others!

Father, heal me so that I can serve You; and
Give Your name glory, in Jesus' Mighty Name!
Thank You for hearing my prayer! I love You!
AMEN!

(Isaiah 65:24)

Healed

I'm healed in Jesus' name!
The promises of His Word, I faithfully
Claim!

I'm healed! Your power and glory is
Revealed! To Your Spirit, my heart
And mind congeals—

And by Your Spirit, I'm filled, healed,
And continually sealed!

Your truth and righteousness is
Continually being revealed! Your power
And glory builds!

Thank You Jesus, I'm healed! You pull
Down principalities and evil powers that
Produce doubts and fears!

In my renewed spirit, praise God cheers
Rise above the enemy's gears!

I'm physically and spiritually healed; You
Wipe away my brawny tears!

Hallelujah! I'm healed in body and soul!
I'm a valued member of Your holy fold! To
Your will and way, I'm totally sold!

I'm healed! So, I stand holy, righteous,
And bold!

In Jesus Christ, I'm a redeemed and
Blessed soul! Hallelujah! Praise God!

(Jam. 5:14; 3 Jn. 1:2; Rev.21:4)

Jesus

J=Justified by faith in the Holy Word

E=eternal life comes through His shed blood

S=salvation is through Christ's dedication to love

U=unity with the Father Who looks down from above

S=sanctified and Secure by the indwelling Holy Spirit!

The love of Jesus has no limits or bounds!
His grace and mercy surround and continue
To fall down!

(Jn. 1:1-14; 3:16; 6:38-46; Acts 4:12; Rom. 5:1; Jer.
31:3

You Are

Lord, You are my Father, Savior, and my
Best Friend to the end!

In every trial and test of life, I know that
You will keep me and defend!

You are faithful and just to forgive my
Sins, over and over again!

I'm so grateful and thankful for Your Holy
Spirit, who lives within!

You supply everything that I need! Your
Word of Truth, I daily heed!

Every day of my life, I desire You to guide
And lead!

You quench my thirst; my hungry soul, You
Feed! You strengthen me to do good deeds!

You are my all in all—my everything! You
Train my heart and soul to joyfully sing!

Melodies of eternal love and salvation, You
Bring! Lord God, You make my heart and
Soul beam!

Your amazing grace is radical and extreme!
Only You have the power to redeem!

(Neh. 8:10; Rom. 5:11; Phil. 4:13; Rev. 1:8; 22:12-14)

Promise Keeper

Lord, You are our Promise Keeper!
For, what You say, You'll surely do!
Your Word and way are faithful and true!

You promised to aid and rescue all who
Choose and follow through on what You
Tell them to!

Your promised David that he would be
King, but for many years, he experienced
Rejection, fears, and jeers!

But when the time was right, the promise
Was fulfilled—his heart was filled with
Happiness and cheers!

Lord, You are our Divine Promise Keeper!
We put all faith and trust in wonderful You!
You teach us what and how to do!

We are confident that Your will and way
Are true; and in all we go through, we'll be
Drawn closer to You!

Trials and tests, You allow! Over time,
They endow with blessed assurance that
You are our Promise Keeper!

Lord, You've never failed to keep a promise!
To You, Jesus, we give our all! We wait to
Hear Your divine call!

You are the Promise Keeper—within Your
Love, grace, and mercy, You allow us to
Grow deeper! Thank You Lord!

(2 Sam. 5:1-25; Ps. 21:5; Jer. 29:11)

I See You Jesus

I see You Jesus! I see Your hand at work in
The world and in my life!

My wrongs, You are helping me to make right!
Please, keep holding my hand—hold it tight!

Each day, You give me wisdom and strength to
Fight the *good fight!* You are my Holy Delight!

I see You Jesus! Your hand of mercy and grace
Stare me in the face!

Your unmerited favor, I experience in so many
Flavors! You change my questionable behavior!

I was once lost! In You, I'm found! I can love
Those who are hateful to me and low-down!

I can come alongside them to help when, in their
Own selfishness, they start to drown!

You teach me how to love unconditionally—this is
The call to freedom and liberty!

I see You Jesus! Your love and kindness surrounds!
Your power and glory continue to stream down!

The wonder and awe of You is profound! Bells of
Joy and melodies of love linger around!

In Your Holy Presence, Your power and glory resound!
Your Shekinah Glory replay Your Story within my heart
And soul!

I see You Jesus! You died and rose! You live forever!
You opened flood gates and allow love and hope to
Pour!

One day, I'll stand at Heaven's door; and I'll see You Face to face! In the Spirit, I behold You now! Praise The Lord—I can see You Jesus!

(Jn. 4:12; 6:46; Acts 7:55-56; 1 Tim. 1:17)

Amazed

Lord, I stand amazed! I'll praise You
All my days!

Your grace and mercy truly amaze! On
Heavenly things, I focus my gaze!

For a new standard of grace and mercy,
Within my soul, You raise!

Lord, You truly amaze! Let the whole
World give You ecstatic praise—

You amaze! And I stand amazed as I
Fall at Your feet! Only You make me
Complete!

I hang out at Your mercy seat—continual
Praise and worship, I daily repeat!

Jesus, You amaze! And the awe and
Wonder of You keep me amazed! May
Your name forever be praised!

(Jn. 3:16; 2 Tim. 1:9; 2 Pet. 1:2; 2 Jn. 1:3)

Eternal And Immortal

Oh Lord, You are eternal and immortal!
You are the invisible God!

You live within each repentant heart! You are
The One True God! You live in me! You give
The victory!

I give You praise and thanksgiving, and all of
Me! You open blinded eyes to see wonderful
You!

You, oh Lord, are always faithful and true!
Your Word teaches us what to do!

Lord, You make us free! You are our Divine
Jubilee!

You are eternal and immortal! I trust in You
With all that I am!

You give us the blessings of Abraham! And all
Whom You bless cannot be dammed!

Jesus—eternal and immortal is who You are!
You are also our Bright and ever Shining Star!

Hallelujah—praise the Lord, from every nation
And all creation! We bow to the eternal and
Immortal Savior, Lord, and God!

We worship and praise You Jesus! For all the
Good we can ever do, You are the reason!
Thank You!

(Jn. 3:16; 1 Tim. 1:17; Rev. 1:8)

Part Four

Intimate Worship

Wait Patiently

I wait patiently for You oh Lord! You are the
Strength and joy of my life! Lord Jesus, You
Are my life!

You are my necessary food for body, soul, and
Spirit—a life without You, I don't care to live it!

When I look back over my life and reflect on
Where You brought me from—Lord there is
Nothing I can't overcome!

When my soul is low and downcast, I reflect
On the past! I recall the hope You give—*"My
Child abundantly live!"*

These words to my heart are so real! All my
Enemies and foes I continually forgive due to
The peace, joy, and contentment, I feel!

So, into our quiet and secret place, away I
Steal! For great is the love, and the never
Ending compassion, You give!

It never fails! Your kind care is new everyday!
Great is Your faithfulness unto me! It never fails!

The good news of Your unending love, grace,
And mercy, I faithfully and joyfully tell!

Lord, You are my portion! I wait for You every
Day of my life! You are my Forever Living
Sacrifice!

Lord, I seek Your Holy Face! I wait patiently for You—
You are so good to all who genuinely seek You!

I wait quietly in Your holy presence! Thank You for
Saving and keeping me everyday! Lord, I love You
Too!

(Lam. 5:19-26; Ps. 27:14)

Wait On The Lord

Wait on the Lord; and be of good courage!
He will give strength to your heart!

Put all your faith and trust in Holy God!
He is your Rock and Strong High Tower in
Every hour!

Trust the Lord and lean on His mighty and
Everlasting power!

Blessing after blessing, He continues to
Shower! Trust Him; and under the weight of
Trials and troubles, you won't cower!

Wait on the Lord! In all you face, rest in, and
On, His amazing and radical grace!

Trust His Holy Word and pray! In His holy will,
He will strengthen you to stay!

Wait on the Lord; and yield to His love—multiplied
Blessings will surround you from above!

Wait on the Lord! Bask in His forever and eternal
Peace, joy, hope, and love!

Always give thanks, worship, and praise to the
Lord! Pray and find strength to stay in God's Holy
Way! WAIT ON THE LORD!

(Ps. 9:10; 27:14; 56:3-4; Isa. 12:2; 40:31)

He Is There

God is there! As you turn to the left or to the
Right! He is there to assure you that He does
Care!

Each burden that you have, He will share!
He is there! His love and concern—He'll declare!

He is there with you in the midst of the sorry and
Pain! Through it all, His love and compassion
Remains!

He is there! Allow Him to help you bear your pain
And sorrow that human understanding can never
Explain!

Give your all to Jesus! He is there to wipe away
Each tear! So, when life's circumstances are not
Clear—remember God is always near!

And when trials come that you don't understand,
Squeeze His hand; then trust His holy plan!

Jesus is the God-Man! And in all you face, He
Enfolds you in His amazing and radical grace!

Find peace in knowing that He is there; and is
With you everywhere! Praise the Lord!

(Jn. 14:27; Rom. 8:38-39; Isa. 41:10; Zeph. 3:17)

Hard Pressed

When I'm hard pressed on every side,
I rely on You to lead me and guide!

Your truth and righteousness within me,
I cannot hide!

For, I do trust You to meet all my needs;
Because You always provide!

The Spirit purges and cleanses me from
Without and from within!

Lord, I ask You to forgive me of all my
Sins!

Make me over, and give me power to be
Renewed again and again!

When hard pressed, I can come boldly
To the Throne of grace—at your feet, I'm
Blessed!

Trials and troubles come and sorely press!
But You allow them to bring forth my best!

Dear Lord, only You can give real peace
And sweet rest from every trial and test!

All my sins, I confess! Only in You, Jesus,
Do I find hopeful peace and calming rest—

Even when I'm not hard pressed! In You
I'm wonderfully blessed! Thank You!

(2 Cor. 4:8-12)

Discouraged

Don't be discouraged or dismayed
When things come in to disturb the
Peace within your soul!

Just remember whose hand you hold!
You are a valued member of God's
Fold!

In Him, you'll find peace and rest, as
He allows you to be brave and bold!

The indwelling Holy Spirit is within
You to give comfort as He consoles!

When discouraged, just know that in
The love of Jesus Christ, you are an
Abundantly blessed soul!

Go to God's Holy Word—for, it's there
That the full story is told! Rejoice!
And again, I say rejoice and be glad
In Jesus' mighty name!

New hope, peace, and joy, you can
Claim! Jesus is always there! On
Your life, He has eternal claim! His
Love is forever and always the same!
Thank You Jesus! I love You Lord!

(Jer. 29:11; Jn. 3:16; 14:27; Phil. 4:4-8,13)

Thank You For The Whisper

Our God is an awesome God! He holds us at the
Center of His heart!

In all we go through, He is always there! He
Intercedes for us and He does truly care!

Our burdens and heavy loads, He does share!
When we are unsure; and don't know what to do,
He's our Divine-Go-To!

In stress and unrest, God will whisper to your
Heart—*Be still My child! Rest! Wait on Me!*

*I Am with you and I will lead you; and will faithfully
Guide—every need, trust Me to provide!*

Just a whisper from the Lord at the right time, and
Your spirit, with His Spirit, will align!

Jesus is mine; and I'm His! All that I need to survive
And thrive, Jesus Christ gives, and the Holy Spirit
Builds!

All that we need, God gives and reveals when, by the
Holy Spirit, we are sealed! My brother and my sister,
Be filled in Jesus' name! Amen!

(1 Ki. 19:11-13; Ps. 139:23-24; Matt. 10:27)

Take Time To Pray

If today is a very busy day, take time to pray!
Ask Jesus to lead and guide you along your
Journey's way!

In all you do, He will keep you on task when
You focus on Him and pray!

So, take time to invite the Lord to orchestrate
Your day—to guide the things you do and say!

For, He knows every turn and bend in the road
You trod! He knows the condition of your heart!

Pause to pray! Hear what the Lord and Savior
Has to say! Allow Him to energize your day!

Take time to pray! Let the 'Son-shine' illumine
Your way! Jesus Christ is the *only* way!

Thank You Father for the Son! Each day teach
Us to make time to pray! Thank You for today!

(1 Thess. 5:16-18)

Your Words

Inner power yields outward control that can
Curse or bless your soul!

Your words have power to create or destroy!
To bring sorrow or joy!

Your words can give you control or render
You out of control—thus a miserable soul!

Your words can become humble, yet bold!
So, seek to bless other living souls!

Your words can be arrogant, self-centered,
Harsh and cold! But they still shape and mold!

What do your words speak? What do you seek?
Being humble doesn't mean being weak!

Do your words speak kindness and respect?
Gentleness, yet firm?

Are your words deceptive, selfish, and quick to
Condemn others, so you'll have your way?

Pause to think on how your words affect your
Life and others too! In the end what you give will
Return to you!

For, your words have power! They speak what's
In your heart! What do your words say?

(Prov. 4:23; 15:4; 16:24; 18:21; Matt. 15:19)

Something Within

There is something within that pushes me onward
When my faith grows thin!

There is something within that keeps me when I
Confront trouble around life's bend!

I'm strengthened to keep going when I'm surrounded
By temptations to yield to various sins!

There is something within on which I can total depend!
Each victory, I can win!

Power rises up within me when I pray, study the Holy
Word; then apply the truths I know!

Something within continues to rise up and grow! And
A renewed faith in God starts to bestow!

God's power and love, I feel! His grace and mercy is
Real! The Holy Spirit is the eternal seal!

Thank You Jesus for the *Something within*—it's the
Power of wonderful You! Hallelujah! Praise God!

(Jn. 3:16; 14:26)

I Hunger And Thirst

I hunger and thirst for God's righteousness!
At His throne, I long for His holiness!

All that He has done for me fills my heart with
Gratefulness!

His grace and mercy takes away fear, doubt,
And hatefulness! I'm filled with thankfulness!

I will always hunger and thirst for Jesus because
He gave me second birth!

Jesus is God's Only Begotten Son! Only by and
In Him was salvation done, and eternal life won!

I hunger and thirst for Jesus, my Christ! For my
Sins and the world's, He paid the ultimate price!

Jesus Christ died, rose, and forever lives as our
Reigning Sacrifice!

I hunger and thirst for God's goodness, mercy,
And grace! One day, I'll behold Christ face to
Face!

I'll hunger and thirst no more when I enter His
Divine and peaceful shore! I'll praise God
Forevermore!

(Matt. 5:6; Ps. 119:2)

When I'm Weak

When I'm feeling weak, it's the love of Jesus
That I seek!

When I'm weak, God makes me strong! I hear
The melody of a joyful song!

Peace and love fills my heart as I'm drawn
Closer and closer to Holy God!

When I'm weak, at the Throne of Grace, I go!
At His feet, I bow low!

God's grace and mercy, the Holy Spirit of God
Does bestow!

And stronger in faith and trust, my spirit will grow;
For I know that Jesus loves me so!

When I'm weak, only God can make me strong,
As I trust in Jesus' name! For when I'm weak,
Then I'm strong! Thank You Lord!

(2 Cor. 12:10; Phil. 4:13)

Far Spent

My day is far spent, for I can see God's
Finger prints guiding my day along the way!

I pause to reflect as I pray! This is a blessed
Day! I claim it in Jesus' name!

The day has just begun; yet it's far spent—in
My spirit, I have the Lord's daily blueprint!

So, I will not allow the unknown and unexpected
Things to prevent my worship and praise!

The day has just begun, yet it's far spent because,
By God, I've been sent to proclaim His love!

Jesus is the Way, the Truth, and the Life! This is
His true story that reveals His glory!

Jesus Christ alone saves lost souls! We all must
Tell His story! For, the day and the way are far
Spent! Go and tell it in Jesus' name!

(Ps. 19:1; Jn. 1:14; 14:6; Phil. 4:19-20; 2 Cor. 4:6)

The Little Things

Give God thanks for all things, especially the little
Things!
Numerous joys they often bring; causing the heart
To happily sing!

Take time to reflect on the little things of life! God
Could be speaking golden nuggets of advice!
For, He has a plan and purpose in all He allows—
Even in minute things God's wisdom endows!

The little things that God gives can speak volumes
To the heart and mind!
He can speak joy and peace—can teach us, to
others; be loving and kind!

Slow down and enjoy the little moments of life that
Have no price—but are precious in God's sight!
They remind us to do right!

So, slow down, pause and stop—listen for God!
Taste His morsels of wisdom as they drop!
A renewed soul and spirit, the enemy can't prevent
Or stop!

Steal away with God; and see the little things that
Make life big and grand!
Take His hand and use Godly wisdom to work your
Life's plan!

Be grateful and thankful for the little things, and the
Joys they bring!

(Heb. 12:28-29; 13:15-16; Ps. 7:17; 9:1)

Through It All

Through it all—the trials and tests, the ups and
Downs, and all the rest; God hears me when I
Call!

He prevents fatal falls—I trust and depend on the
Lord through it all!

I fast and pray! I study His Word and obey! He
Sends angels to guide my steps each day!

When I'm about to give in, God's blessed assurance
Kicks in! His truth and righteousness defends!

The love and grace of God fills my heart! Through
It all, I trust Him; and on Him I totally depend!

I daily thank the Lord for His love; for He graciously
Cares! I continually say thank You for the blessings
He always shares!

In all I go through in this life and in the one to come, I
Know in my spirit that my Savior, Lord, Master, and
Lover of my soul is there! He will be there to the end!

(Jer. 29:11; Matt. 2819-20)

Save All

In life there will be trials and tests!
But, in Christ these serve as a means
To bless! So, in God, find peace and
Sweet rest!

The Father gave us His very best, so
That we might live and experience
Eternal success!

Trust in God! Give Him your heart;
And eternal peace and hope will never
Depart!

Receive the seed of salvation! Allow it
To grow deep within—Christ's blood
Takes away sin!

Open your heart and mind and let the
Savior in! Jesus came to save us all!

Hear and accept His loving call! The
Holy Word and prayer are the cure-all!

Trust and obey in faith! It leads to that
Secret and sacred place in the garden
Of amazing and radical grace!

Jesus came to save us all! Go! Tell
The world—*Jesus will pick you up, if
You fall! Believe in Jesus' name!*

(John. 3:16)

Plant The Seed

Sow a seed in the ground!
With faith and love press it down!

Live, love, and serve others—show kind
Compassion to your sisters and brothers!

Plant the seed by meeting another's needs!
Daily water your seed with faith and trust!

Tell all you meet that the blood of Jesus
Was poured out at His mercy seat!

In Jesus, there is no defeat! Faithful service
To Him will allow you to rise above defeat!

Plant the seed that God placed within your
Heart—see the residue of the love of God!

When the seed takes root, it brings forth
Blossoms of love, mercy, peace, and hope!

All the weeds of trials, sorrows, pains and
Disgust will bring a fragrance of godly trust!
In all you face you'll divinely cope!

Plant the seed, so in others, it will awaken
Salvation's need—then hungry souls, God
Will feed!

Keep sowing the Gospel seed! It meets
Soul-stirring needs! For the Kingdom of
God is at hand!

Serve! Continue to work God's plan! Plant
The seed in the ground of your heart, so that
Eternal life can be found in Jesus' name!

(Eccl. 11:6; Matt13:20; Mk. 4:14)

Fleeting Of The Night

The night is fleeting! Wrong decisions, many
Souls keep repeating!

Time is running out! *Today is the day of
Salvation—harden not your heart!*
Make up your mind to fall in love with Jesus—
He is Holy God!

Time is fleeting! The ways of this world are
Stressful and defeating!
But, Jesus Christ is the answer! Go tell a dying
World that the night is flying away! Stop and
Pray!

Jesus promised a new day, and a better way!
The night is fleeting!
Without Jesus in your heart, your life is empty
And defeating! Awake from your sleep, and
The love of Jesus, desperately seek!

For, God honors the desires of the humble
And the meek! Wake up! Get up—for the
Night is fleeting!

Darkness is flying! Too many people are dying!
Loved ones are left behind grieving and crying!
Come to Jesus! For, time is running out!
Choose this day whom you will serve! For, the
Night is far spent!

The Remedy has been sent—choose Jesus the
Christ!

(Matt. 6:33; Rom. 6:23; 10:9-10; *2 Cor. 6:2*; 1 Thess.
5:16-18;
2 Pet. 3:9; *Josh. 24:15*)

Don't Rush

Don't rush! Take time to feel the brush of
Angels' wings!

Angels are all around! God uses them to
Shower blessings down!

Don't rush! Take time to talk to God, so He'll
Build up your trust! This is a must!

God is always there with You, even in your
Darkest hour! He gives you His strength and
Power!

Don't rush! Stop! Reflect upon His love and
Kindness! He won't leave you alone! He is
Never gone!

Don't rush! But instead, hunger and thirst for His
Presence and goodness!

Don't rush! For God desires to spend quality
Time with you! He lives within us!

And as you study His Word, take time to meditate
And pray; then obey! Allow Him to guide you in
His holy way!

Don't rush! In His forever love and care—totally
Trust! It's a must! Don't rush!

(Ps. 91:1-2; Matt. 19:26; Jn. 14:27; 2 Tim. 1:7; Heb.
7:25)

Broken To Be Mended

We are broken! Our Creator allows it, so that
We can be mended!

For, our doubts and fears are continually
Contended, but within us, they are defended!

We judge ourselves and others by what we feel
And by what we think we see!

But, life is often not the way things appear!
Therefore, our vision and focus are unclear!

Only when we start to develop '*forever eyes*' do
We start to plainly see how God sees us!

In God, we must give total trust! But, we often
Mistrust and continue to divide and fuss!

Each of us is broken! Sin is the token! It divides
And seeks to conquer!

But through the love of Jesus, we have strength,
And a reason to come together in love!

Jesus said: "*Love one another as I have loved you!*"
We all are broken, but through the blood of Jesus,
We are made whole!

By faith, the Holy Spirit mends every hurt and flaw
In Jesus' name! Trust God, and obey—He will
Guide your way!
We are broken to be mended!

(Jn.16:33; 17:21-23; Rom. 12:12; 1 Pet. 1:7, 9)

Blessed Through Tests

Our Creator knows exactly what we need!
He knows what diet to feed!

So, at the right time and in the proper serving
Size, God allows trials and tests to advise!

So, to our life, His truth and righteousness,
He applies! His grace and mercy is in disguise!

Trials and tests are allowed and designed by our
Creator to bless and not to stress!

For, we are drawn to Him in the midst of life's
Unrest—God knows what's best!

So, to Holy God—go! All your sins and doubts, to
Him, confess! He will give you peace and rest!

Read and meditate on God's Word! This is how
You get to know Him! He doesn't condemn!

Pray to the Lord daily and throughout the day!
Ask Him to guide your way!

Trials and tests are designed by God to bless—all
Your sins confess!

To become more like Jesus is how we pass our
Tests! Obey, grow, and be blessed in Jesus' mighty
Name!

(Prov. 3:5-6; Jn. 15:16; Rom. 5:3-4)

Freedom

Freedom afterwhile! Lord, allow us to walk
Together; and rise above the hatred and guile!
For I know one day we'll see You, and will live
In royal style!

Help us to seek unity and not division! Help us
Make kind and wise decisions!

Freedom is free to all that can see You—Your
Mind and heart which proves You are a loving
God!

Freedom afterwhile! Help us to make it a
Reality and not a denial!

Help us to cling to the peace and hope we
Receive through the birth of the Christ Child!

Help us seek freedom regardless of the hew of
The skin, or the neighborhood that we live in!

Compel us to seek God's truth and righteousness—
And discard political and ethnic foolishness!

Help us to focus on Jesus—His love and holiness,
Then we'll be blessed with a desire and will to
Seek and find freedom! Freedom will come
Afterwhile!

(John 8:36)

The Sweetest Name

Jesus is the sweetest name I know!
He saved me and helps me grow!

His love, grace, and mercy upon me,
He graciously bestow!

He lifts me up when I feel sad and low!
He opens each closed door!

Jesus teaches me to love Him and
Others more and more!

Upon His own, Jesus' grace, provision,
And protection, He will continue to pour!

Jesus is the sweetest name I know!
He's holy, loving, and kind—He is mine!

Jesus is forever the same! His promises,
I claim!

Jesus, He's the reason for all the good
I do! With His love, grace, and mercy, He
Does pursue!

Jesus is powerful and mighty in all His
Ways! His name commands our worship
And our praise!

Jesus—let all Heaven and earth proclaim!
A touch from Jesus, and we won't be the
Same!

Jesus! Jesus! Jesus! Your name, I forever
Proclaim! It's the sweetest name that I
Know! Jesus, I love You!

(Jn. 14:13-14; Phil. 2:10-11)

Don't Quit

Don't give up and don't quit!
God invites you to come to His mercy
Seat and sit!

At His feet, allow the Holy Spirit's fire,
Within you, to be lit!

The Lord will empower you to give the
Devil a Holy Ghost fit!

Just don't quit! But do fast, pray, and
Study the Holy Writ!

For, by fear and doubt, you are not
Eternally bit—don't quit! Move forward
And embrace God's benefits—

Power and courage to serve, you'll
Discover in reserve—God will keep you
And give you what He deems, you
Deserve!

Don't give up or give in—for this is sin!
But allow the Spirit to motivate you from
Within!

On Jesus totally depend! He forgives
Sin and will move you to a desired end!

So, don't quit! Trust and obey Holy God,
And you'll receive His eternal benefits—

His love, peace, joy, and His power in
Your meekness! Trust God and obey!
Be assured that help is on the way! Don't
Ever quit!

(Jer. 29:11)

We Can't

We can't but God can as we start and
Continue to abide by His holy plan!

He has already given us His divine
Command! It's written down in the
Precepts of His Holy Word!

It's through God's truth, obeyed, that
His voice is heard! And in obedience,
God's power undergirds!

We can't serve the Lord on our own!
But we can succeed when we put active
Faith and trust in God alone!

He will lead, guide, and teach us right
From wrong!
For, He promised never to leave us on
Our own!

We can't succeed or effectively lead
Unless we cast all our cares on Jesus
Christ alone!

We can't, but God can, as we study,
Pray, and choose to work His plan!
Reach out and take His mighty hand!

Daily live and serve as God commands!
Then you'll soon discover, you can't do
The impossible, but God truly can!

Hallelujah! Thank You Lord! Every day,
You assure me that I can work Your
Holy plan!

(Ps. 77:14; Jer. 32:27; Matt. 17:20; Lk. 1:37; 18:27;
Phil. 4:13)

On My Way Home

I'm on my way home!
And the last mile, I'll have to walk
Alone!

But, I'm not on my own! Jesus, Your
Spirit is with me in each step I take!

I'm assured of Your Words—"*I Am
With you and I will never forsake....*"

I'm on my way home! I draw nearer
Every day! Lord, I hear You when I
Pray!

In Your holy presence, You encourage
Me on my journey's way!

I'm on my way home! All doubts and
Fears are gone! I can hear Heaven's
Joyful tones!

Lord, I'll delight to hear You say:
"*Servant, well done.*" This would be the
Added bonus of unending joy!

I'm on my way home! Thank You, Lord!
Thank You, Jesus for Your undying
Love!

(Jn. 14:6; Jer. 29:11)

Born To Live

We are born! We live; then we die!
We leave loved ones to mourn and cry!

Show and help us to live as You desire!
Fill us with Your Holy Fire!

Holy Spirit live in me! Continue to set
Me free!

Father, open my eyes, so Your glory I'll
Continue to see!

Twice born, my soul and spirit turn from
Doing wrong to doing right—

Lord, You teach us to be holy in Your
Sight! By faith, we fight the good fight!

And in all we do, Jesus Christ is our Holy
Delight!

We are sealed by Your Holy Might—thank
You Holy Spirit!

We are born to live! The glory of the Son,
The Father gives; by His Spirit, we are filled
And healed!

In the great name of Jesus, we are born to
Eternally live with and in Him! Amen!

(Jn. 3:16; Col. 1:27)

Accept It

Accept what God allows, so that His power,
In you, He endows!

He knows best what you need! Trust Him!
And let God lead!

All that's not wholesome and good, He will
Turn it around; so, it'll work out as it should!

Accept what God puts on your plate! His
Provisions, we learn to appreciate!

Daily, on His Holy Word, meditate; and your
Mind and thoughts, with His truth, saturate!

Accept what God allows, even when you
Can't understand His holy plan!

Keep holding on to God's hand! Do as He
Demands!

Accept what He allows! Make up your mind
By faith—accept it, in Jesus' name!

(Eccl. 3:1; Prov. 16:4; Matt. 19:26; Rom. 8:28)

My Life Is Christ's Life

When Jesus came into my heart, I
Died to the sins of willful pride! I chose
To allow the Holy Spirit to lead me and
Guide!

By faith and trust, I invited the Lord
Inside! All my needs, He promised to
Provide!

No good thing from His own servants
Will be denied! And His divine wisdom
And revelation, He won't hide!

I live my life by the power in Jesus' name!
His truth and righteousness, I desire to
Claim! His Spirit renders me not the same!

The life I live, I live by faith in Jesus Christ!
He is the Father's One and Only choice!

In faith I hear and obey God's voice! My
Life is no longer my own; but the love and
Hope of Jesus lives in and through my life!

I live, but yet not I! For Jesus Christ lives
In me; so that I might become all He
Desires of me! In Christ, I'm set free!
Praise the Lord!

(Rom. 6:1-14; Gal. 2:20)

Trust

Don't let your heart be troubled!
Trust in God! Give Him all your heart!

For, He delights to give you the desires
Of *your* heart!

Give your all to the Lord! Trust Him and
Obey! And from the truths of His Word,
Don't stray!

Read and study God's Word every day!
Fast and also pray—be faithful, come
What may!

Trust in the Lord; for God loves you with
An everlasting love! He sent His Son from
Above!

Allow Him to fill your heart with *His* love!
Be sensitive to the leading of God's
Heavenly Dove!

Jesus offers love, peace, joy, and hope!
In all you face, He'll allow you to cope!
Just believe! *Trust* in the Lord!

(Prov. 3:5-6; Jn. 14:1)

Be Careful

Be careful about what you say and do;
For the residue will cling to you!

And over time it will reveal what's within
Your heart that's real and true!

For, what you give out, will one day return
Back to you!

Make sure that your words are faithful
And true! Only seek to duplicate what
God renders to be His purpose for you!

Trust God and pray! Be assured that He
Will aid you and rescue! Be mindful of
What you say and do!

So, be careful! Allow God's Word and
Faithfulness to be a guiding light for you!

(Rom. 5:8; Ps. 7:16)

Safe

I'm safe in the arms of God!
Each day, He draws me closer to His
Heart!

In His Holy Word, He promises that
He will never part—He lives within my
Heart!

If I remain true and faithful, I'll receive
My eternal reward! I'll live forever with
Him! He won't condemn!

No power in the heavens, on earth, or
Below can stop God's blessed flow!
In His arms I go, as my soul and spirit
Start to glow!

Safe in the arms of Jesus is the only
Place I desire to know! He loves me
So!

I love Him too! He is the faithful One,
That's eternally true! Jesus, thank You!

(Isa. 41:10; 53:1-12; Jn. 14:3)

The Blessing

The blessing is in the pressing!
Each day I press toward the mark of
The high call!

In the midst of the struggles, God won't
Let me fall! He is the greatest power of
Them all!

The blessing will prevent the stressing!
Open your mouth—all your sins, begin
Confessing!

If you are a child of God, start living and
Possessing your divine blessing!

The blessing is in the atmosphere! Press
On to the mark! And to the voice of the
Holy Spirit, hark!

God won't let you down! Blessing after
Blessing in His presence are found!
Surrender all to God and behold His
Blessings falling down!

His blessing enfolds you in every round!
You discover that God's grace is profound!

So, experience His power and blessings
That set free the captives, once bound!
Eternal salvation is profound! Hallelujah!
Praise the Lord!

(Jn. 3:16; Philp. 3:14)

God Is

God is your Source of life, strength, and
Power!

Without Him, you can't live—not even for
An hour!

Your whole being and health relies totally
On God's power and your state of mind!

God is your high protective tower that keeps
You when prone to cower.

Trials and tests can zap your will-power! You
Can find strength in Holy Spirit power!

To pray, worship, and serve God, with a pure
Heart, is all you need in Jesus' name!

(Jer. 29:11; Jn. 3:16)

God Loves

This one thing I know—God loves you from
The gutter-most to the utter-most!

By faith in God, believe and receive the Holy
Ghost!

God's eternal love will make you brand new—
At the cross, He came to your rescue!

Read and meditate on His Holy Word; for it
Teaches you what you should do!

Don't you know? Are you not convinced?
At Calvary Jesus came to your defense!

God's love was put on display for all the world
To see! It was given to save and set you free!

God loves at all times! But to reject so great
Of a love is the eternal crime!

God's love demands a choice! Which will you
Choose? Eternal life with Him or eternal
Death without Him? Receive His eternal love!

(Jn. 3:16; Rom. 5:8; Gal. 2:20; 1 Jn.4:9-11)

Jesus Christ Lives

Jesus Christ lives! His life for yours and mine,
He came to give! The wages of sin, His shed blood,
Forgives!

Look up to the cross; believe and eternally live! For,
By His stripes, we are healed!

By His death and resurrection, the power and grace
Of Holy God is revealed!

Christ eternally lives! His love and righteousness,
He came to give! He lives! The Holy Spirit fills and
Eternally seals!

Trust Him and obey; and eternally with Jesus, you
Will stay!

Love Him and others—He won't let you stray, as
You pray each day!

(2 Cor. 13:5; Jn. 14:19)

In Jesus' Name

There is no reason to worry or fear,
When in the name of Jesus Christ
You revere!

In Jesus' name, your steps are made
Clear! A vision of your destiny will
Appear!

In Jesus' name, His truth and
Righteousness are yours to claim! He'll
Help to make your way plain!

For, only in the steps of Jesus are you
Able to find peace and joy in the midst
Of sorrow and pain!

Even in the struggles with disappointments
And regrets; in His name you'll experience
Eternal gain!

Trust in God! Give Him all your heart!
He dispatches angels to protect you and
Stand on guard!

For, all you'll ever need, do, or see that is
Good and glorious—it's met in Jesus' name!
Praise the Lord!

(Luke 10:17; Jn. 1:3; Phil. 2:10; Col. 1:16)

The Lord Is There

The Lord is there with you!
He will see you through each trial
You go through!

He truly loves you!
Wait on Him; and He will renew
You!

His love is forever true and He will
Never abandon you!

But you must believe and trust
That the Lord is there with you;
For, the Holy Spirit lives in you!

(Isa. 40:31; Jer. 31:3)

Grace And Mercy

God's grace and mercy suits the case!
I'm given all I need to run my life's race!

God allows me, at times, to determine the
Pace!

For, it's conditioned on how faithful I run
My race!

Each trial and test that I face, my God is
There—His victory to declare!

And His power and might to an unbelieving
World, I stand to declare in Jesus' name!

God's grace and mercy renders me, not
The same!

In the midst of heartache, sorrow, and pain,
Total surrender to the purpose of Holy God
Is eternal gain!

God's grace and mercy is available to one
And all—claim it in Jesus' name!

(2 Cor. 9:8; Eph. 1:7; Hob. 4:16)

Breaking Chains

I hear the sound of chains breaking! My God is
Moving me to step out and engage in spiritual
Risk-taking!

A new creation within me, He is making! He leaves
No room for me to continue faking!

God's truth and righteousness within my soul and
Spirit is breaking! And of His grace and mercy, I
Keep partaking!

Chains are breaking down that once held me bound!
Wisdom and power, in my God, is found! Jesus is
There to pick me up when I fall down!

As I get up, I pause and look around! Blessing after
Blessing, from God, surrounds—to praise and
Worship God, I'm lovingly bound!

The chains of fear, doubt, and oppression no longer
Hound! I'm free in Jesus!

For, the chains have fallen in Jesus' name! Thank
You Father God, Holy Spirit, and Jesus, my Lord and
Savior, and soon to return King of kings!

Jesus, oh what peace, joy, love, and hope, to my heart,
Only You can bring! I open my mouth to You in praise
And I sing! Hallelujah! Hallelujah! Hallelujah any how!

(Jn. 8:34; Heb. 2:14; Rom. 7:24; 6:18; Jn. 3:16)

You Will Rise

When trials and tests press you to the ground,
By faith in God, they can't keep you down!

In Jesus' name, you will rise because the
Faithfulness of God is what you prize!

For the Spirit of God lives on the inside!—He
Leads and guides!

He keeps in stride your selfish pride—but seeks
The good of other, to provide!

You will rise because You keep Jesus Christ as
Your closest Friend and constant Guide!

He alone gives you hope, peace, joy, and love
Each morning on the wings of Heaven's Dove!

You will rise when you allow the Lord God to
Advise—yield, and let the Holy Spirit supervise!

He will revive body, spirit, and soul; and in the
Image of God, He will mold!

Do as you are told; and you'll be a blessed soul!
For, you will continue to rise by faith in Jesus'
Name!

(Phil. 3:13-14; Titus 2:11-14)

Part Five

Praise For All Seasons

Be Thankful

In all things, be thankful and grateful—never be
Resentful and hateful!

Remember all that the Lord God has done for you!
In your good behavior and in your bad—He
Remained faithful and true!

And when things were hard, He stepped in to defend
By giving you encouragement to contend!

Be thankful! Be content and grateful! In all that God
Allows, focus on how these tests were helpful!

God knows you better than you do! He seeks to show
You His grand version of you!

Be thankful for what He brings you through! He seeks
To open your eyes and heart, so that you'll desire it too!

Be thankful for what God does and the things He allows!
With His love and kindness, He endows!

Remember, God elevates the humble and bring low
Those with selfish greed and self-centered pride! From
God, there is nothing you can hide!

Be thankful, generous, and helpful to those in need! And
No good thing from you will be denied!

Be thankful! Be grateful! His blessings, He will bestow
With endless flow! Thank You Jesus! Thank You God!
I love You with all my heart!

(1 Thess. 5:18-19, 23)

Give Thanks

Great God
Invisible & Invincible
Victorious
Eternal

Trustworthy
Hope
Almighty
Nurturing
King
Sovereign

(1 Thess. 5:18)

Thanksgiving

Trust in God

Hope in God

Almighty presence

Never alone

Kindness and love

Safe in God's protection

Great is His faithfulness

Individual and personal care

Victory over life struggles

Indwelling Holy Spirit

Nurturing prosperity

Goodness and mercy of God

(Ps. 100:4; Ps. 107:1)

Two Hearts

Two hearts have become one; and
By the love of God it was done!

A new life together has begun!
So enjoy your life together and have
Fun!

Keep loving each other and trusting
In Jesus Christ, God's only Begotten
Son!

Open communication with each other
Is how each victory is won!

Two hearts beat as one because of
God's Son!

Husband and wife communicate, and
Keep loving each other!

(Mark 10:9)

Father

Faithful to God & Family
Affectionate & protective
Trustworthy & True
Holy & Humble, not prone to grumble
Emotions grounded in God's love
Resourceful & Resigned to God's will!

(Ps. 103:13; Prov. 22:6; Malachi 4:6)

A Father

A father loves at all times! He teaches
His children to love others and be kind!
He shows by example how to live and
Serve God, the Divine!

He loves his family; and sacrifices for
Them! His children love and respect him!

A father teaches godly character by how
He lives; and by the godly example that
He gives!

He teaches them to live for God; love, and
Others, forgive!

A real father has the heart of Holy God; and
Holds the Lord in high regard!

(Ps. 103:13; Prov. 22:6)

Mother

Merciful—toward the situation/needs of her child.

Open—to various ways God can teach, and grow her child.

Thoughtful—regarding the purpose and design God has for her child.

Helpful—willing to see that her child develop God's full potential.

Encourager & **Eager**—to love, share, and encourage others to love God.

Resourceful & **Resolute**—to seek and see the good and best in her child.

(Prov. 1:8-9; 31:25-28; Lk. 1:46-48; 2:51; 3 Jn. 1:4)

Mother's Day

Mother's Day is a special time of year
When the children gather far and near!

They come to celebrate and honor the
One who is so dear! The one who taught
Them to serve God with a pure heart!

The one who was always there to wipe their
Tears and calm their fears!

She taught them how to act and behave,
And gave needed discipline when they
Misbehaved!

She was a firm believer in: *Spare the rod,
You spoil the child!*

She gave them encouragement to do and be
Their best; and she still support them in their
Quest!

She makes them feel that they are the best!
And in her eyes, they outshine the rest! She
Impresses upon them just how much they are
Blessed!

So, on this special day, her children come
Together to celebrate and honor her—the one
Who gave them birth!

Her children come with words and acts of love—
For her children, everyday is Mother's Day! So
They gather this day to say:
We love you mom! HAPPY MOTHER'S DAY!

(Prov. 31:28; Lk. 1:28)

A Mother's Love

Nothing can compare to a mother's love!
It is a love that was fashioned by God above!

It has no limits or bounds—it defies human
Logic and is rare when found!

A mother never gives up on her child, no matter
What comes or what seeks to beguile—

Whether her child is right or wrong—that's still
Her child; she'll seek to correct all the while!

A mother's love goes beyond human reason!
But to some it may seem like societal treason!

There is a bond of love that is stronger than
Death, health, or wealth! She will love her child
With her last breath!

A mother's love will sacrifice for the welfare of
Her child—even to the point of rational denial!

But a mother's love must be balanced by the
Love of God—His love is what cushions the
Heart! It sets the redeemed apart!

A mother's love must be balanced by God's
Love—He so loved that He gave all!

When a mother's love comes from the heart of
God—it brings, love, peace, and joy that lives on
Throughout generations!

A mother's love should imitate the Father's
Love!

(Prov. 31:28)

Mama

Mama, I think of you often, but especially
Near and during Mother's Day celebration!

I remember your love and gentleness that
Was balanced by your strong tenderness!
And when the need arose, firm discipline,
You imposed!

I remember how you took time to talk with
Me when I wanted to do wrong—especially
That one time when I was grown, and on my
Own—*Don't pay wrong with wrong,* is what
You taught!

And based on God's Word, I knew it was
Best to do what I ought!

I love you mama! And I miss you so very much!
I miss hearing your voice, seeing you smile,
And embracing your tender touch!

But amid my occasional tears, God gives me a
Smile, as I remember the talks we shared while
You made so many things clear!

You lived a life of love and compassion toward
Everyone! You taught me how to live, forgive,
And give as Jesus taught!

And over the years, the truths of God were
Caught! And now your life is portrayed in me—
All because, I saw Jesus Christ in you! This is
What you taught!

God's love is real and true—it's seen in what
We say and do! I seek to do what God tells
Me to—mama, it's all accredited to you!

Thank you, mama, for showing and telling me
What God would do! I pause to say to you:
I miss you and wish you were here!
HAPPY MOTHER'S DAY! I LOVE YOU MAMA!

Remembering Your Grandmother

I know just how precious a grandmother
Can be! My grandmother was there for me!

For, God's amazing grace allowed your
Grandmother to be in your life and in your
Heart!

Always cherish the memories of those days,
As you reflect and give God a thank You
Praise!

Though she is away from your presence, she
Lives on within you! And at any moment, you
Can affectionately think of her too!

Rest in the Lord and in His peace; and your
Joy will be complete; until such time, again
You will meet on Heaven's table land!

So, fully live your life, because Christ paid the
Price! Amen! Amen! Amen!

(Eph. 6:2-3)

Joy To The World

Joy to the world, Jesus Christ was born!
Let the heavens and the earth rejoice!
To eternally live with Him, we now have a choice!
Lift your voice and joyfully proclaim—Jesus, the
Christ Child is born!

For, He came from above to give, joy, peace, and
Unconditional love! Joy to the world, Christ came
To give! A new life, He wants us to live! Receive
Him in your heart—Jesus Christ is the Son of God!

Joy to the world and to all who receive Him in their
Heart! Go! Proclaim the joy that this world cannot
Destroy! For, God became a human being—now
The Father's glory can be touched and seen!

Joy to the world, Christ the Savior was born! God's
Eternal power and glory was wrapped in the person
Of a little baby boy! And in the shadow of a cross,
Jesus was born to give eternal life and joy, so that
Many, by faith, would live!

At Calvary's Hill, the God-Man, Jesus Christ, would
Be lifted high! He was born to die, so that we could
Live!

Joy to the world—the Father gave His Own Son to
Bear our sins! Grace and mercy He chose to give!
Go and live; and to others, forgive! Believe, receive,
And in Jesus Christ totally trust!

Joy to the world, for the Savior of the world has come!
Lift your voice and joyfully sing—new hope, sweet
Peace, love, and eternal salvation He came to give!
Joy to the world, Jesus eternally lives and gives!
Praise the Lord!

(Ps. 16:11; 98:1-9; Isa. 9:5-6)

Jesus Is The Reason

Jesus is the reason for the season!
It's a season of love!

So, every season is a reason for love
Because Jesus came down from above!

Born as a little baby in Bethlehem! He
Came to give peace, life, and joy!

So, give Jesus your heart—know that He
Is God in human body form!

Invite Him in, and your mind and heart, He
Will transform!

From God, the Father, "a Child was born
And a Son was given!" To all who believe—
Their sins are forgiven!

Jesus is the reason that we have a relationship
With the Father! He is the only way to be saved!

To every believer, give Him hallelujah praise all
Your days!

Jesus was born; and He grew to become the God-
Man! He is the Mediator of the Father's plan!

With nails in His feet and hands, upon a cross, He
Paid it all for our sins—

By His blood, we win—He rose with all power; and
Is coming back again—He takes away sin! He is
The reason in every season! Love personified is
Who He is!

Eph. 1:18-19; Rom. 8:28; 1 Jn.4:14; Jn. 4:42)

Bethlehem

Oh little town of Bethlehem—
Within you, was born God's
Little Lamb!

He came to give hope, peace
And joy to all who will believe!
Open your heart and receive!

See the Baby Jesus lying in
His manger bed!
In a stable, on hay, He laid His
Little head!

By a star, the wise men were led!
And the shepherds believe what
The angel said!

So, the prophecy came true
That said: "*Christ the Savior is
Born!*" And one day, on His head,
A crown of thorns will be worn!

Bethlehem, oh Bethlehem, we
See the Christ Child!
Born so that, for our sins, He
Would die!

Trust in God! Trust in Jesus!
For on the power of His Holy
Spirit we can rely!

Bethlehem! Bethlehem! Behold
The Lamb, the Lamb of God!
Invite Him into your heart!

Matthew 2

Happy Birthday Jesus

Happy Birthday Jesus!
We gather to celebrate Your Special Day!

I have no gift to bring, except the praise songs
We, together, sing!

Joy and happiness, to my heart, You bring! I
Thank You for everything!

Jesus, I know You love me; and I love You too!
Teach me how to please You!

When I'm sad, You help me feel glad! You are
The Best Friend I've ever had!

Jesus, You were born! You grew up! You died,
Upon a cross!

Jesus, You rose from the dead, so that we would
One day, forever live with You!

All You say is true! So, I choose to do what You
Tell me to!

I have no gift to bring; but I give You all of me!
Thank You Jesus! Thank You Lord! I *Love You*!

HAPPY BIRTHDAY JESUS! It's the Best Birthday,
Ever!
                    (Luke 2:7-20)

Jesus Is The Gift

Jesus is the Gift that keeps on giving!
It's seen in our daily living!
His gift is not limited to December 25th!
For everyday His love gives us a lift!

He calls us to do the same for each
Other! His love and joy, we can claim
Everyday!

Let others see God's gift in you each day!
Point them to Jesus' way! Show love and
Care by what you do and say!

Read the Bible and pray! Jesus will guide
Your way! Remember, Jesus is the Gift,
That keeps on giving 24-7!

Let others see the gift in you—Jesus truly
Loves you! He wants you to show love
To others, and not just at Christmas!

Jesus is the reason for every season!
Thank You Jesus for Your love everyday!
HAVE A BLESSED DAY AND NEW YEAR!

(Isaiah 9:6; John 3:16; 15:12)

Wise People

Wise people still seek Jesus! This is
The season to seek after God!

God gave His Only Begotten Son—
Jesus Christ!

By faith receive Him—invite Him into
Your heart!

For, He is the only way to please Holy
God!

Jesus Christ was born beneath a star,
But in the shadow of a cross—

His love and sacrifice paid sin's debt,
And defeated all that is evil and false!

See the sweet baby Jesus asleep on the
Hay—His destiny points to God's way!

As God-Man, He would fulfill the Father's
Plan! By faith, trust Him and obey His
Commands!

Christ the Savior and King is born—wise
People still seek Him! Do you?

(Prov. 3:7-9; Isa. 9:6; Jn. 3:16)

A Manger Bed, A Cross

In
A manger bed
The little Baby lay His
Little sweet head!
He came to give the world a
Choice to be spiritually fed!
Baby Jesus lay in a straw bed!
By love He was led! He was born
To die upon a tree, to set believing souls
Free! He came to live, die, and rise—to give us
Liberty! Sin and death, by Him, will cease to be!
He came to give believers the gift of eternal life—
He came to die! Then He rose! Jesus, forever lives!
By the Holy Spirit, He fills! His love and grace builds! We
Celebrate gifts under the tree! But the Greatest Gift of all hung
Upon a tree! Praise God for the gift of His Son!
HAPPY BIRTHDAY JESUS
MERRY CHRISTMAS, too!
YOU ARE THE REASON! WE LOVE WONDERFUL YOU!

(Isa. 9:6; Jn. 3:16)

Happy New Year Jesus

Happy New Year Jesus!
This I claim in Your mighty name!
Nothing will be the same—

New-found strength and power, in You,
I claim! It's a new year and a new way to
Glorify and serve You!

More of You, I'm able to give when less of
Selfish me, live! Holy Spirit, my soul and
Spirit—please fill!

All my soul and body diseases, I ask You to
Heal—greater faith, hope, and trust, build!
By Your Spirit, I'm sealed!

Happy New Year Jesus!
I'm here! You are the reason! More of You
Is my heart's desire!

As I decrease, You will increase within my
Heart and spirit—my spirit with Your Spirit,
Testify!

I must die to myself; and on You totally rely!
For, one day my spirit will take to the sky; for
Now the truth of Your Holy Word, to all I meet,
I'll share!

Happy New Year Jesus—all year because, I
Know You are there! This truth, I'll boldly
Declare! Thank You! Happy New Year Jesus!

(Matt. 28:20; Jn. 10:10; 14:27)

Easter

E-ternal life in Jesus Christ
A-fter-life forever with Him; He paid the price
S-alvation of the redeemed soul—more precious
than gold
T-rust and faith in His story told—we stand bold
E-verlasting joy and hope, the Spirit, molds
R-esurrection power and relationship with God,
bestowed!

HAPPY EASTER DAY!
RESURRECTION IS EVERYDAY!
JESUS LIVES FOREVER!
AMEN!

(Matt. 28:6, 18; Lk. 24:6-7; Jn. 11:25;
1 Cor. 6:14; 15:3-4; 1 Pet. 1:3; 13:3-4)

Upon A Cross

Upon a cross, He hung until all life, from His
Body, was rung!

The Son of God hung between earth and sky—
For your sins and mine, He came to die!

By this sacrifice and act of love, eternal life for
The world was won!

By Jesus Christ, the Son of God, this act of love
Was done! For, He was the *only One* who could!

Because of love, the Son knew He should; and
The Father decreed that He would!

So, upon an old rugged cross, Jesus Christ hung,
Bled, and died! And upon Him the sins of the
World were tried!

Eternal death and the grave, Jesus defied! Look
Up to Calvary and faithfully live!

Trust and believe, and everlasting life, you'll receive!
Jesus Christ forever lives! Allow Him to live in you!

(Acts 4:12; Gal. 1:15-16)

Calvary's Hill

They led Jesus to Calvary's Hill
It was there that His blood was spilled,
And God's glory revealed!

From His brow, side, hands, and feet
It looked like defeat! But for us it was
An invitation to worship at His mercy
Seat!

God's mercy and grace is revealed on
Each redeemed face!

Jesus has gone ahead to prepare us a
Dwelling place!

For, Jesus came to serve and not to be
Served! A ransom for our sins, we did
Not deserve!

Love is the motive for all God does! And
The love of God to other we must give!

(Mk. 10:45; Jn. 3:16)

The Power Of The Cross

The scene at the cross appeared to be
God's weakest hour! But, in reality, it was an
Hour of miraculous power!

For, it was God's finest hour! Upon an old
Rugged cross His Son hung! Life from His body
Was rung!

God's love and mercy were completely done
Through the shed blood of His Son!

Jesus Christ died and rose to protect and save
Us from eternal harm! Over Satan, death and
The grave, Christ's resurrection gave power to
Overcome!

And to all who believe, into the family of God,
Everyone is welcomed!

By the power of the cross, death and the grave
Were tossed! The Spirit of God reveals all that's
False!

The power of the cross has no limits or bounds!
For everlasting life, peace, joy, hope, and love
Are found! Thank You Jesus for your endless
Love! All power rest in Your hands—the Father's
Plan!

(Jn. 3:16; Rom. 1:16-1 7)

Jesus, My Hero

Jesus, You are my Hero; and I put all my trust
In You! I walk where You tell me to!

Jesus, You are my Hero! You walk with me
Everywhere I go! Divine grace and mercy, You
Bestow!

You lead me out of valleys, low! You guide my
Steps up mountains, winding and high!
You give me courage to press on when I'm afraid
To try!

Because of Your great love, I choose to comply!
In Your goodness, I'm persuaded to do Your will
Or die!

Jesus, You are my Hero! You lift me high when I
Humbly bow low!

I'm reminded of how much You love me so—to die
Upon a cross, You were destined to go!

Eternal life is for all who believe by faith and receive—
Salvation that You came to bestow!

Thank You Jesus for the Holy Spirit Who resides in
Me—setting me free!

You rose from the dead so all can see—You are the
Savior of the world—Jesus, You are my Hero!

(Prov. 3:5-6; Heb. 11:6)

Graduate

Great joy that you feel within

Resolute that the best is yet to come

Aware of a job well done

Determined to be the best that you can be

United in who you are and what you want

Appreciative of family and friends

Trusting God to guide your path

Eagerly anticipating your future!

(Jeremiah 29:11)

Sunset

Every day is an opportunity to come
And sit at the Master's feet—a daily
Holy Retreat!

He allows us time to see and reflect:
"Lord, You are the One Who cares
And protects!"

He gives us sunny days and many
Chances to give Him praise!

And on cloudy and stormy days, we
Still come before Him with holy hands
Raised!

Always give reverence to the God
Who is the *Ancient of Days*!

For in each life, the sun will set!
Let it be with peace and hope and not
Regret!

Trust in Jesus and let His Spirit, your
Life, control!

For, one day, your spirit and soul will
Take flight to its final abode!

Every sunset is preset to bring you
Face to face with Jesus Christ—the
One you *must* truly know!

He invites you to bask in His eternal
Glow!

(Jer. 29:11)

When Heaven Calls

When Heaven calls, our attention is
Put on pause! For the love of Jesus
Is the cause!

When we pray, in the will of God, we
Ask to know His heart everyday!
We trust and rely on Holy God to order
Our steps! By Him, we are kept!

When Heaven calls, we stop and
Pause—waiting for nuggets of truth
And wisdom to fall!

When Heaven calls, we stop and
Listen for words of love and peace
From our God!

He knows each heart and gives what
We need! He knows the proper diet
To feed—His truth and righteousness,
We must heed!

As Your Shepherd, allow Jesus Christ
To lead! And be attentive to what you
Hear!

Draw near to the Lord, so that what you
Hear will be clear when Heaven calls!

Lord, I hear! You are always near!
Draw me nearer to Your bleeding side!

I love You! Each day, I patiently wait
For Heaven's call!

(Jeremiah 33:3)

I Am With You

When confusion rolls in like fog, and
Troubles rush in like a mighty flood,
Remember God's Word:
I AM with you always!

Trust My Word and obey! Never
Cease to pray! My Indwelling Holy
Spirit is here to stay!

Never stop calling on My name!
For My promises, you can claim!

Draw near to Me and I will be near
You! Know in your heart that all I
Say is true! I AM with you!

In every storm, and through the
Rain, My faithfulness remains!

I'm there to banish your doubts and
Fears! To keep you, as the storm
Cloud clears!

Always know—never doubt that, *I AM
With you!* So trust and do as I tell
You—

And in due season, I will come to
Your rescue! For My eyes never
Leave you!

I see you! By faith, know that *I AM
Always with you!*

Matthew 28:20

Precious Memories

Precious memories, how they linger
They are guided by God's finger!

Fond memories of loved-ones passed
Won't allow you to linger and be sad!

For God gives memories to make you
Glad and hold you fast!

Precious memories allow the company
Of family and friends to last!

Refreshing as a melody from above!
God blesses us, to have them so the
Heart remains full of love!

Precious memories, how they linger
Thoughts and memories won't depart
Because dear loved ones are blessings
Directly from God; and they return to God!

Precious memories warm the heart and
Draw us closer to Holy God!

(John 3:16; Song of Solomon 2:1)

Closing Thoughts To Ponder

- The Christian Life is not about how much Scripture that you know, but rather how much you apply in your daily life.

- Belief that has no action is really unbelief!

- God's Word is a mirror! When applied to daily life, it reflects the love of God.

- Believers do not demand respect, but command it by the way they choose to live.

- Submission and obedience to God never goes unnoticed or unrewarded by Him.

- Ultimate power and authority come from God; and those who misuse it will eventually answer to Him.

- Be grateful that God I committed to bringing out your very best in every life test.

- Life is not so much about what you go through, but more about how you go through—what you learn and what you do.

- Sometimes your greatest asset can seem as if it's your greatest liability.

- You cannot force anyone to become who they are not willing to be. Real change comes from within.

- "Without faith, you cannot please God" as Scripture says. But without love, there can be no real faith.

- When you discover that you can do nothing without God, you will begin to succeed!

- Keep trusting and believing; and the blessings of God, you will keep receiving.

- God is on your side; expect Him to provide!

"We walk by faith and not by sight."
(2 Corinthians 5:7)